HISTORY

SERIES TITLES

ASIAN CIVILIZATIONS
was created and produced by McRae Books Srl
Via del Salviatino, 1 — 50016 — Fiesole
(Florence), (Italy)
info@mcraebooks.com
www.mcraebooks.com

Publishers: Anne McRae, Marco Nardi
Series Editor: Anne McRae
Author: Neil Morris
Main Illustrations: Giacinto Gaudenzi pp. 35, 37;
Giacinto Gaudenzi and Alessandro Menchi pp. 10–11;
MM comunicazione (Manuela Cappon, Monica
Favulli) pp. 8–9, 22–23, 27, 28–29, 43, 44–45;
Alessandro Menchi pp. 40–41; Leonardo Meschini pp.
20–21, 31; Paola Ravaglia pp. 14–15; Claudia Saraceni
pp. 6–7; Sergio pp. 18–19

Smaller illustrations: Studio Stalio (Alessandro
Cantucci, Fabiano Fabbrucci, Margherita Salvadori)
Maps: Paola Baldanzi
Photos: Corbis/Contrasto, Milan pp. 12b ©Richard A.
Cooke, 16–17b ©Lindsay Hebberd, 24–25b ©Asian
Art & Archaeology Inc, 38–39 ©Charles E. Rotkin;
Werner Forman/Art Resource, NY pp. 32b
Art Director: Marco Nardi
Layouts: Rebecca Milner
Project Editor: Loredana Agosta
Research: Loredana Agosta, Claire Moore, Ellie Smith
Repro: Litocolor, Florence

Consultants:

Dr. ALFREDO CADONNA is associate professor at the
department of East Asian Studies at the University
of Ca' Foscari, Venice, Italy.

Dr. GREGORY POSSEHL is an anthropological archeologist
with broad interests in the development of urbanization
in the Old World. His specific research and writing have
focused on the first phase of urbanization in South Asia,
namely in the ancient cities of Mohenjo-Daro and
Harappa. He has been conducting field research and
excavations in India since 1979.

Library of Congress Cataloging-in-Publication Data

Morris, Neil, 1946-
  Asian civilizations / Neil Morris.
     p. cm. -- (History of the world)
  Summary: "A detailed overview of the early history of
American and Pacific peoples, including Native
Americans, Maya, Aztecs, Inca, Aborigines, and the
Maori, up to 1200 CE"--Provided by publisher.
  Includes index.
  ISBN 978-88-6098-160-8
  1. Asia--Civilization--Juvenile literature. 2. Asia--
History--Juvenile literature. 3. Asians--Migrations--
Juvenile literature. 4. Civilization, Ancient--Juvenile
literature. I. Title.
  DS12.M64 2009
  950--dc22

                                         2008008403

Printed and bound in Malaysia

HISTORY

Asian Civilizations

Neil Morris

Consultants: Dr. Alfredo Cadonna, University of Ca' Foscari, Venice, Italy.
Dr. Gregory Possehl, Professor of Archeology, Department of Anthropology,
University of Pennsylvania and Curator of the Asian Section, University
of Pennsylvania Museum of Archeology and Anthropology.

Zak
BOOKS

Contents

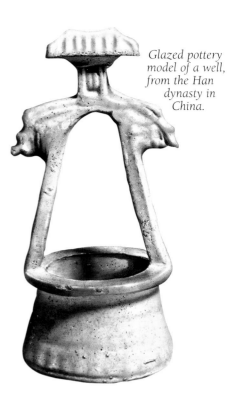

Glazed pottery model of a well, from the Han dynasty in China.

Note—This book shows dates as related to the conventional beginning of our era, or the year 1, understood as the year of the birth of Jesus Christ. All events dating before this year are listed as BCE (Before Current Era). Events dating after the year 1 are defined as CE (Current Era).

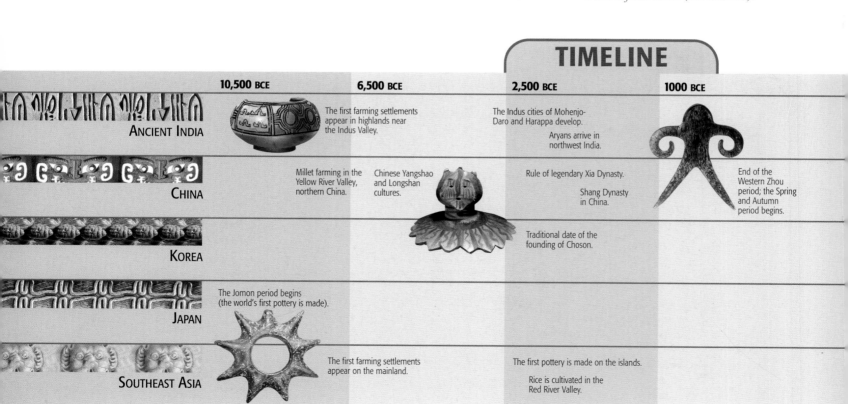

TIMELINE

	10,500 BCE	6,500 BCE	2,500 BCE	1000 BCE
ANCIENT INDIA	The first farming settlements appear in highlands near the Indus Valley.		The Indus cities of Mohenjo-Daro and Harappa develop. Aryans arrive in northwest India.	
CHINA		Millet farming in the Yellow River Valley, northern China. Chinese Yangshao and Longshan cultures.	Rule of legendary Xia Dynasty. Shang Dynasty in China.	End of the Western Zhou period; the Spring and Autumn period begins.
KOREA			Traditional date of the founding of Choson.	
JAPAN	The Jomon period begins (the world's first pottery is made).			
SOUTHEAST ASIA		The first farming settlements appear on the mainland.	The first pottery is made on the islands. Rice is cultivated in the Red River Valley.	

Introduction

Marble panel with Buddhist figures from Gandhara, in the ancient Kushan Empire (present-day Pakistan) dating from the 2nd century CE.

After the descendants of nomadic hunter-gatherers started growing their own crops many thousands of years ago, farming villages grew up in different parts of Asia. Simple settlements developed into important civilizations in great river valleys, such as the Indus Valley in present-day Pakistan and the Yellow and Yangzi rivers in modern China. Rulers founded dynasties, and some small city-states turned into great empires. Wars were fought and rulers rose and fell, but at the same time great progress was made in art and technology. This was also true in Korea, Japan, and Southeast Asia, where Chinese influence was great. Our look at early Asian civilization ends around 1,500 years ago, when a variety of cultures were flourishing throughout the continent.

Burnished pottery bowls and other vessels from the Yayoi period in Japan.

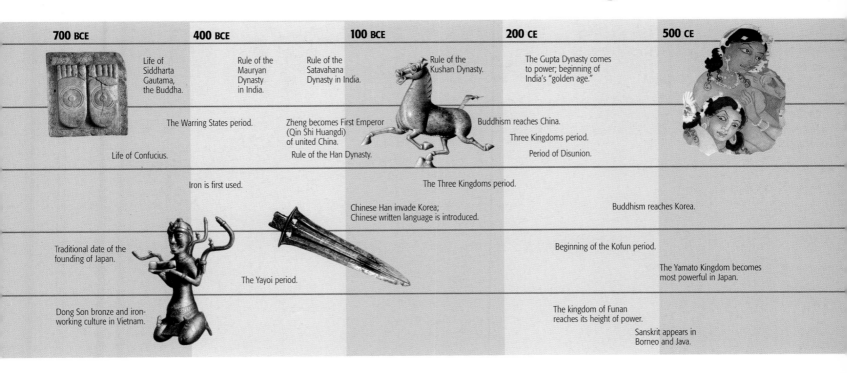

700 BCE	400 BCE	100 BCE	200 CE	500 CE
	Life of Siddharta Gautama, the Buddha.	Rule of the Mauryan Dynasty in India.	Rule of the Satavahana Dynasty in India.	Rule of the Kushan Dynasty.	The Gupta Dynasty comes to power; beginning of India's "golden age."	
	The Warring States period.		Zheng becomes First Emperor (Qin Shi Huangdi) of united China.	Buddhism reaches China.	
	Life of Confucius.		Rule of the Han Dynasty.	Three Kingdoms period. Period of Disunion.	
	Iron is first used.			The Three Kingdoms period.	
			Chinese Han invade Korea; Chinese written language is introduced.	Buddhism reaches Korea.	
Traditional date of the founding of Japan.				Beginning of the Kofun period. The Yamato Kingdom becomes most powerful in Japan.	
		The Yayoi period.			
Dong Son bronze and iron-working culture in Vietnam.				The kingdom of Funan reaches its height of power. Sanskrit appears in Borneo and Java.	

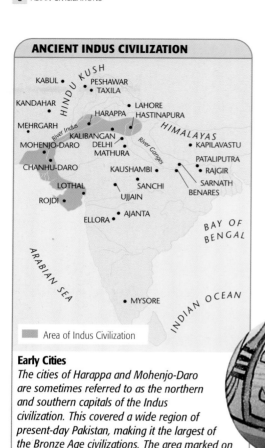

Area of Indus Civilization

Early Cities

The cities of Harappa and Mohenjo-Daro are sometimes referred to as the northern and southern capitals of the Indus civilization. This covered a wide region of present-day Pakistan, making it the largest of the Bronze Age civilizations. The area marked on the map above shows the area of Indus Civilization and the major sites.

Origins of Indus Civilization

Around 7000 BCE the descendants of Stone Age hunter-gatherers were settled in the hills to the west of the Indus River. There they began to grow cereal crops and domesticate animals. By 6000 BCE people were farming on the plain that was watered by the great river and its tributaries, where the soil was enriched by the annual flood. Farming settlements grew into villages and towns, and two large cities developed and flourished for many hundreds of years.

Pottery and Jewelry

The earliest Indus art included terra-cotta figurines, mainly of young women wearing jewelry but also of bearded men. Potters made massive storage jars, water pitchers, and smaller decorated vases, which were all fired in large kilns. Craftworkers made intricate jewelry, especially necklaces and other items of small soapstone beads. They also used gold, silver, and gemstones imported from surrounding regions.

A decorated bowl, with a typical black-on-red design.

A metal balance scale and set of weights from the Indus Valley.

Weights and Measures

Indus traders used stone weights carved into cubes. These were standard throughout the region. The basic unit was 16, and weights varied from tiny cubes used for measuring spices to large blocks for weighing metals.

This necklace was found among other grave goods in Mehrgarh.

This terra-cotta amulet shows an Indus boat.

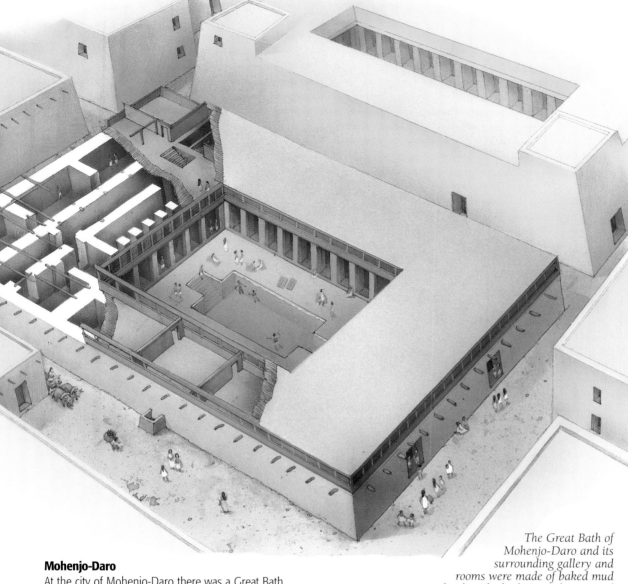

INDUS CIVILIZATION

7000 BCE
Farming begins in the highlands to the west of the Indus Valley.

6000 BCE
People begin to farm on the Indus floodplain; earliest pottery and use of copper.

3500 BCE
Development of small towns; craftworkers start using the potter's wheel.

2600 BCE
The plow is used in the Indus Valley; the cities of Mohenjo-Daro and Harappa develop.

2500 BCE
Cotton cloth is woven at Mohenjo-Daro. Development of Harappan script. Bronze is used to make weapons and tools.

2400–2000 BCE
Height of the Indus civilization.

2350 BCE
Trade with Mesopotamia.

2300 BCE
Harappa and Mohenjo-Daro grow to a population of up to 35,000 each.

1900 BCE
Indus civilization undergoes a great transformation. Cities are abandoned and people return to a simpler lifestyle.

The Great Bath of Mohenjo-Daro and its surrounding gallery and rooms were made of baked mud bricks. The bathing pool measured about 39 x 23 feet (12 x 7 m) and was more than 8 feet (2 m) deep.

Mohenjo-Daro

At the city of Mohenjo-Daro there was a Great Bath symbolically elevated on a mound and surrounded by a colonnaded gallery and important buildings. Historians believe that the bath was used for ritual bathing, perhaps before worship in a nearby temple. The city had a network of wells, and most houses in the residential district had washrooms and lavatories which were connected to drains running beneath the streets.

Clay model of a cart pulled by two oxen from Harappa.

Indus Agriculture

The annual Indus flood created good conditions for farming. The main food crops were wheat and barley, and some farmers also grew rice and cotton. There were domesticated cattle, sheep, goats, pigs, asses, and fowl, and hunters may have chased deer and other game on the grasslands beyond the floodplain.

This Indus spearhead is made of copper. Other tools were made of bronze which was made by mixing copper and tin.

City Planning

Mohenjo-Daro was a well-planned city, with streets laid out in a grid pattern. It was made up of two sections: a mound, where there were important public buildings (see page 7), and a lower district of ordinary residential houses. Though close together, the houses were quite separate, with an entrance off a quiet back lane rather than the busy street.

Cutaway reconstruction of a two-storey mud-brick house at Mohenjo-Daro. It was built around a central courtyard, and people probably spent a lot of time at roof level, where there was plenty of light and air.

Religious Beliefs

We know little about Indus religion, but figurines have been found that are thought to represent a mother-goddess. She may have been accompanied by a male "great god," and both were probably worshiped at home or in small, local shrines. No large temples have been found in the cities, but experts believe that busts of bearded men may represent priests or kings.

This limestone head of a bearded man may represent an Indus Valley priest-king.

Writing

People of the Indus Valley had their own writing system, which was made up of pictographs. This was used by traders on the thousands of stone seals that have been found. The seals were probably used to identify goods, but experts have not yet been able to decipher the script.

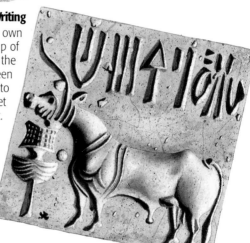

Carved soapstone seal from Mohenjo-Daro, used to mark clay tags for goods. Unfortunately we do not know what the short inscription means.

BRONZE STATUETTES

As well as terracotta figurines, artists produced excellent cast-bronze statuettes. These represented carts and animals, as well as dancing girls. The bronze girl shown here wears only a necklace and bangles on her arms. The girl's posture suggests a dance, which was later to become an important part of Indian temple ceremony.

This bronze statuette is just 5.5 inches (14 cm) tall.

Life in the Indus Valley

From finds at Mohenjo-Daro and other sites, we know how Indus Valley cities were laid out. We also know something of how people lived in the Indus civilization. But we still have much to learn about their social and political organization. The cities had buildings that may have had a religious or ceremonial purpose, and historians believe there was an important class of priests. But no palaces have been found.

Trade

The Indus people traded near and far. Local merchants went from city to city, bartering the goods that they carried overland by pack animal or along the river by barge. Those that ventured further afield obtained metals such as gold, copper, and lead from the surrounding highlands, and gemstones such as lapis lazuli and turquoise from Persia. The port of Lothal, on the Gulf of Cambay, was used for sea trade with Ur and other Mesopotamian city-states. Cotton textiles provided one of the most important Indus exports.

Terra-cotta mother-goddess figurines from Mohenjo-Daro.

Reconstruction of a busy street in Mohenjo-Daro, where farmers brought their wheat and barley to the city granary at harvest time.

The Aryans

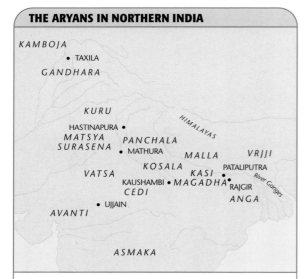

KAMBOJA
• TAXILA
GANDHARA

KURU
HASTINAPURA •   HIMALAYAS
MATSYA   PANCHALA
SURASENA • MATHURA   MALLA   VRJJI
          KOSALA   PATALIPUTRA
VATSA   KAUSHAMBI • KASI •   River Ganges
          CEDI • MAGADHA • RAJGIR
          • UJJAIN   ANGA
AVANTI

        ASMAKA

Around 1500 BCE a new group of people arrived in the Indus Valley region. They came from central Asia and called themselves Aryans. By that time the Indus civilization had undergone its transformation, and the Aryans established themselves amidst the local people of ancient India. The Aryans brought with them the Sanskrit language, and their traditions, hymns, and beliefs gradually developed into the Hindu religion.

Territories

The Aryans came to the subcontinent across the passes of the Hindu Kush mountains. They called the first region they came to, near the Indus, the "land of seven rivers." Each Aryan clan or family group was headed by a warrior-chief. Some groups continued south toward the plains of the Ganges River, where the annual flood was more predictable. This map shows the 16 "great realms" that had developed in northern India by 600 BCE.

This copper harpoon blade may have been for ceremonial use only.

The Aryans

The Aryans brought with them herds of cattle, sheep, and goats. They also brought horses, which were used to pull chariots, and dogs. Their animals provided them with meat and milk, and the Aryans measured their wealth in cattle and horses. They probably subdued and overawed many of the people whose territories they moved into.

Much of what we know about the way the Aryans lived comes from a collection of Sanskrit hymns called The Vedas. *They mention chariot races, games, and dancing. However, historians do not know for sure what the Aryans looked like.*

This pottery bowl is in a style called painted grey ware, which was produced in northern India from 900 BCE.

Religious Poems

The Aryans composed a series of poetic hymns, prayers and rituals dedicated to the proper conduct of ritual sacrifice called the *Rig Veda*. The teachings in this and three other *Vedas* were passed down the generations by word of mouth, until they were finally written down in Sanskrit as more than a thousand hymns. The prayers were addressed to deities called *devas*, or "shining ones", whom the Aryans worshiped under the open sky.

AGE OF THE ARYANS

C. 1500 BCE
Aryans arrive in northwest India.

C. 1400 BCE
The earliest Vedas are composed.

C. 1000 BCE
The Aryans begin working iron.

C. 900 BCE
The Aryans move to the east, down the Ganges Valley, and become more settled. They raise cattle and cultivate barley and rice.

C. 800 BCE
Small tribal kingdoms develop in the Ganges region.

C. 750 BCE
Small kingdoms unite to form larger territories across northern India.

C. 700 BCE
The Hindu sacred writings called Upanishads *appear.*

Sanskrit

This complex language was spoken long before it was ever written down. It is written in a script called Devanagari, which has 48 letters and is written from left to right. Modern Indian languages such as Bengali, Gujarati, and Hindi are based on ancient Sanskrit, which belongs to the Indo-Iranian branch of the Indo-European language family. Sanskrit is still used as a sacred language.

The Aryans believed that every year Indra, the god of rainstorms and war, used a thunderbolt to slay the serpent of drought. For this he was greatly praised and worshiped.

Human-shaped copper figure, made around 1700 BCE. This and similar objects may have been dedicated to the gods.

Fourth-century CE Brahmi inscriptions from southern India. The Devanagari alphabet, which was originally developed in the 11th century CE to write Sanksrit, derived from the Brahmi script. Some scholars believe that Brahmi developed from the script that was used in the Indus Valley until about 2000 BCE.

Hinduism

The great world religion of Hinduism developed in that region from the faiths and philosophies expressed in the *Vedas* of the Aryans. It teaches that the human soul never dies, but is reborn in a continuous process of reincarnation.

The First Dynasties of India

Following the Aryan invasion, many small Hindu kingdoms developed across the Ganges plain and challenged each other for power. During the 6th century BCE two new religions were founded—Jainism and Buddhism—and these spread rapidly throughout the region. Two hundred years later, Alexander the Great, king of Macedonia, led his army to a tributary of the Indus River, but his troops refused to go any further. This allowed a young local warrior to take power and found the great Mauryan Empire.

Carved limestone panel of the Buddha's feet, each inscribed with the Buddhist wheel of law.

Buddhism

The Buddhist religion developed from the teachings of Siddhartha Gautama (c. 563–c. 483 BCE), the son of the ruler of a small Himalayan kingdom in present-day Nepal. After the prince left his father's palace, he set out to discover how ordinary people's suffering could be stopped. He became enlightened when he understood the truth about life, and was known as the Buddha (meaning "enlightened one").

Mauryan Empire

Five years after fighting against Alexander the Great (reigned 336–323 BCE), the young military commander Chandragupta Maurya (reigned c. 321–c. 293 BCE) conquered the kingdom of Magadha in the fertile Ganges Valley. He founded an empire that covered much of present-day northern India, Pakistan, Bangladesh, and Afghanistan. The Mauryan Empire reached its height under the founder's grandson, Ashoka (reigned 273–232 BCE), who expanded into much of southern India. He converted to Buddhism and made it the state religion. After his reign the empire declined. The last Mauryan ruler was assassinated in 185 BCE and the Shunga Dynasty was established.

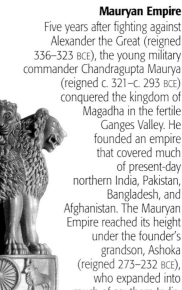

The lion-headed capital (above), with the wheel of law, stood on one of the many pillars put up by Ashoka throughout his empire. It became the emblem of the modern state of India.

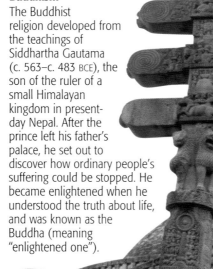

The Great Stupa at Sanchi was built during Ashoka's reign. It may originally have contained remains of the Buddha himself.

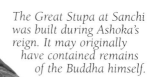

Growth of Trade

The Mauryan capital was at Pataliputra (modern Patna), on the Ganges, and the large empire was divided into provinces. There were good roads between them, and this led to an improvement in trading networks. Craftworkers made items of wood, cloth, and even gold, and the empire traded with Mesopotamia, Persia, and Greece.

This Kushan gold relic-container dates from about 50 CE.

Right: Ivory plaque made by Andhra artisans showing two yakshis, or earth spirits, from about 50 CE.

Satavahana Dynasty

Toward the end of Mauryan rule, a tribal people known as the Andhras came to power in central India. They may have been local officials who gradually became independent rulers, and their ruling family was called Satavahana. The Satavahana defeated the Kanva Dynasty, who had taken over lands of the Shunga Dynasty. The Satavahana, with their capital at Amaravati, became the dominate power in central India.

This Kushan gold pendant of the Greek goddess Aphrodite was found with the remains of a young woman in a Bactrian grave. Showing Greek and Indian influences, the pendant is about 2,000 years old.

The Kushans

The Kushans were a group of nomadic tribes from central Asia. They first conquered the kingdom of Bactria (in modern Afghanistan), before invading northwest India and advancing to the Ganges plain. Their great ruler Kanishka (reigned c. 80–100 CE) became a Buddhist, but the Kushans showed great respect for other religions. They traded extensively throughout Asia, including with the Chinese along the Silk Road, and with the Roman Empire.

Kanishka is shown on this gold coin conducting a fire ritual.

EXPANSION OF THE GUPTA EMPIRE

India Under the Guptas

By the beginning of the 5th century, the Gupta Empire covered the whole of the north and much of the eastern region of the subcontinent. Chandra Gupta I's son, Samudra Gupta (reigned 335–375 CE), made many conquests and adopted the title "Exterminator of Kings;" his southern campaign brought 13 kings and princes under Gupta rule. Later, Chandra Gupta II (reigned 375–415 CE), known as the "Sun of Power," gained more territory in the Ganges and Indus valleys.

- Empire of Chandra Gupta I
- Added by Samudra Gupta
- Temporary tributary to Samudra Gupta
- Added by Chandra Gupta II
- Tributary tribes and states
- Under Gupta influence c. 380–410 CE

A Gupta carving representing the goddess Ganga, the personification of the Ganges River.

This scene, based on a wall painting at Ajanta, shows a raja, a Hindu prince, at his court.

Gupta Origins

We do not know for certain where the Gupta family originated. Many historians believe that the family's homeland was in the region of the Ganges Valley, where they became landowners. From about 240 CE the head of the family was known as a *maharaja*, or prince, and in 305 CE Chandra Gupta I married a princess of the important Lichchavi family, who ruled the kingdom of Magahda.

The Gupta Empire

Detail from an Ajanta wall painting.

The Gupta dynasty of rulers came to power in the northeastern Ganges region, expanding their influence by both marriage and conquest. By 400 CE they controlled a large empire, though the regions furthest from their homeland were allowed considerable independence. The Guptas were followers of Hinduism, and their rulers revived many rituals of the Brahmans, or Hindu priests. But they were also happy to encourage Buddhist beliefs and ways of life.

Wall Paintings

Between the 2nd century BCE and the 6th century CE, Buddhist sanctuaries and monasteries were cut into the cliffs of a narrow gorge at Ajanta, near the southern boundary of the Gupta Empire. The walls of the caves were decorated with wonderful paintings of palaces, forests, and scenes from the Buddha's life.

The entrance to one of the Ajanta sanctuaries shows relief sculptures of the Buddha.

Religious Tolerance

Most Gupta rulers were Hindus, and many were followers of the Hindu god Vishnu (the Preserver). They respected all the other Hindu cults, and people throughout the Gupta Empire worshiped images of Hindu gods and goddesses. Buddhism and Jainism also flourished, however, and the Gupta emperors showed great religious tolerance.

Fifth-century sandstone head of a bodhisattva. According to Buddhist belief, a bodhisattva is a person who has reached enlightenment but stays in the human world to help others.

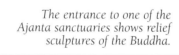

THE GUPTAS

240–280 CE
Sri Gupta heads the Gupta family as a maharaja in the Ganges Valley.

280–319 CE
Ghatotkacha heads the Gupta family.

c. 320 CE
Sri's grandson, Chandra Gupta (reigned c. 320–335), becomes the first great ruler and founder of the Gupta Empire.

c. 330 CE
Chandra Gupta I names his son, Samudra Gupta (reigned 335–375), successor to the throne. Since Chandra Gupta I had many other older sons who claimed the throne, Samudra Gupta spent the first years of his reign putting down revolts.

401–410 CE
A Chinese pilgrim, Fa-hsien (active 399–414 CE), visits India in search of sacred Buddhists texts.

415–455 CE
Reign of Kumara Gupta, who favors religious tolerance and keeps the empire intact.

455–467 CE
Reign of Skanda Gupta, who defeats Hun invaders and resists internal revolts.

467–473 CE
Reign of Skanda's brother, Puru Gupta. The empire starts to decline.

473–476 CE
Reign of Puru's grandson Kumara Gupta II.

477–497 CE
Budha Gupta becomes king. After his death in 497, Gupta lands are divided into many independent kingdoms.

Music

Music, singing, and dance were all important to Gupta culture, and there are many musical references in the works of Kalidasa (see below). It seems that musical performances were given in temple courtyards and theaters. But musical forms were perhaps most developed at the royal court.

Bronze statue of Shiva, in his manifestation as the lord of music and dance. Hindus believe that his dancing moves the Universe.

The mridang *is a double-headed drum that provided the rhythm for early Hindu religious music. It is a very old instrument, appearing on seals from the ancient Indus civilization.*

Centers of Learning

Hindu temples and Buddhist monasteries became great centers of learning during the Gupta period. Students learned about astronomy, mathematics, medicine, and philosophy. Gupta mathematicians invented the decimal system and used Hindu numbers that later became the Arabic numerals used today. The Buddhist center of Nalanda, in northeast India, attracted students from China.

Excavated ruins at Nalanda show some of the monks' cells that were part of the learning center complex.

LITERATURE

During the Gupta period two important Hindu epics, the Ramayana *and the* Mahabharata*, were revised into their greatest Sanskrit form. The famous poet and dramatist Kalidasa (active 5th century CE) is thought to have attended the court of Chandra Gupta II. He was one of the "nine jewels" who wrote great works in classical Sanskrit at that time. Kalidasa's best-known epic poem is called* Meghaduta*, or "Cloud Messenger."*

Fifth-century relief showing a scene from the Ramayana.

Gupta Sculpture

Gupta sculptors were superb stone-cutters, and many of their works were carved in caves and rock shrines, as well as on temple walls. During the 5th century, artistic metalwork reached its peak. Metalworkers cast many images in bronze and copper, especially of the Buddha. A famous rust-free iron pillar commemorated the reign of Chandra Gupta II.

This bronze Buddha dates from around 400 CE.

India's Golden Age

The period of Gupta rule, and especially that of Chandra Gupta II from about 375 to 415 CE, is often called a "golden age" in India's history. Under the Gupta Dynasty learning and scholarship, science and mathematics, art and music, and poetry and drama all reached new heights. The great poet Kalidasa may have been present at the Gupta court, where all the arts were fostered. The culture that developed from the Hindu tradition was encouraged throughout the Gupta Empire.

The End of the Gupta Reign

Around 460 CE Skanda Gupta succeeded in fighting off raids by groups of central Asian nomads known as White Huns. They are also called Ephthalites and are referred to as Hunas in Indian sources. Around the year 500 the Huns defeated the Guptas and conquered northern India. The rulers of some small kingdoms that continued to exist claimed descent from the Guptas, but the successful reign of this great dynasty was over.

Late 5th-century silver coin of the White Huns, who imitated local currency in the lands they conquered.

EARLY CHINESE CULTURE

c. 7000 BCE
Millet farming in the Yellow River Valley, north China.

c. 6500 BCE
Rice farming in the Yangzi Valley, south China.

c. 5000–3200 BCE
Yangshao culture.

c. 5000 BCE
Millet is cultivated around the village of Banpo, near present-day Xian.

c. 4000 BCE
Jade is used to make ornaments and weapons.

c. 3200–1800 BCE
Longshan culture.

c. 3000 BCE
The potter's wheel is introduced in China; evidence of plows being used.

2700 BCE
Possible first weaving of silk.

c. 2500–2000 BCE
First casting of bronze ornaments and tools.

2207–1766 BCE
Traditional dates of the legendary Xia Dynasty.

1766 BCE
Traditional date of the founding of the Shang Dynasty.

c. 1600 BCE
Possible origins of pictographic writing.

Reconstruction of a kiln from Banpo c. 4500 BCE. Pots were placed in a separate chamber above the fire.

Lid of a pottery vessel, dating from about 2500 BCE. It shows a human head, possibly that of a shaman.

Early Potters

At Banpo, there was a pottery-making area beyond the ditch surrounding the village. The pots were shaped by hand, until the potter's wheel was developed around 3000 BCE. The potters' area included six simple kilns, where the clay pots were fired. Heat from the firing chamber baked the pots hard, and their red surface was painted with black designs after firing. Some designs were of animals, others were geometrical patterns.

This bulging terra-cotta pot, dating from about 2200 BCE, was painted with a toad-like design.

In the village of Banpo, near the Yellow River, farming families lived in mud-plastered pole houses with reed-thatched roofs. The village also had a large central longhouse.

Early China

Chinese agriculture and civilization developed around two great rivers. The Yellow River (or Huang He) was named for the color of its mud and clay, which made dry, fertile land for growing millet. Further south, the even longer Yangzi River (or Chang Jiang) flowed through a wetter landscape that was ideal for cultivating rice. Successful farming villages gradually grew into towns, the population increased, and by 2000 BCE a large region was being governed by powerful dynasties.

YANSHAO AND LONGSHAN CULTURES

Yellow River

• LIJICUN

SUFUTUN •

• DONGXIANG

BANPO •

YELLOW SEA

• SANXINGDUI

River Yangzi

▨ Shang bronze working	── Yangshao culture 5000–3200 BCE
╱╱╱ Rice farming 6500–300 BCE	── Longshan culture 3200–1800 BCE
➤ Spread of rice farming	● Shang city

Fertile Lands
The Yangshao culture developed beside the fertile banks of the Yellow River and its tributaries. Farming villages were surrounded by fields of millet, and the villagers also kept pigs. Later, the Longshan culture developed in the same region and covered more territory to the south and east, where the wetter conditions allowed farmers to grow rice as well as millet. As the map shows, rice cultivation developed to the south, especially around the River Yangzi.

Xia and Shang Dynasties
There is no historic record of the Xia Dynasty of rulers, which has become mixed up with ancient myths and legends. Some tell of a heroic ruler called Yu the Great, who supposedly restored the course of the Yellow River after flooding. Certainly we know that the river constantly changed course in ancient times. The first documented dynasty—the Shang—was founded by a ruler named Tang in or around 1766 BCE.

Tortoise shells such as this, as well as animal bones, were used by Shang priests to foretell the future. Questions and answers were inscribed on the shell.

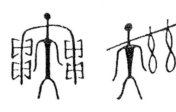

Early Writing
The earliest Chinese writing was produced during the Shang period, but the exact date is not known. Picture symbols were used to represent objects, but many of the pictographs were written on wood or silk, which have not survived. By about 1450 BCE they were being inscribed on oracle bones (and shells) and bronze vessels.

Some examples of early Shang pictographs.

THE SHANG ERA

1766 BCE
Traditional date when founder Tang overthrows the last Xia king, Chieh.

c. 1700 BCE
Production of bronze vessels.

c. 1557 BCE
Zhengzhou becomes Shang capital.

c. 1400 BCE
The Shang capital moves to Anyang.

c. 1350 BCE
War and hunting chariots come into use.

c. 1200 BCE
The Shang king proclaims himself human counterpart of the supreme deity.

c. 1050 BCE
Shang king, Di Xin (reigned c. 1068 – c. 1050 BCE), is overthrown by the Zhou king Wu (died c. 1056 BCE).

The Bronze Age

People of the Shang period were great workers in bronze (an alloy of copper and tin). Craftworkers melted the metal in a pottery crucible and then made casts by pouring the molten metal into clay molds. They used bronze, which is harder than copper, for ritual vessels, weapons and armor. Skillful Shang craftsmen also used jade for utensils and jewelry.

Spearhead with a jade blade attached to inlaid bronze.

Shang Society

The region ruled over by the Shang Dynasty centered on the middle reaches of the Yellow River. Historians believe that there were about 30 successive kings and that their capital moved several times. Royal ancestors were worshiped, and they in turn were thought to mediate on behalf of the living king with the supreme, divine ancestor Shang Di, the "Lord on High." On his death, a king went to heaven to join his great ancestor. The precise year in which the Shang Dynasty came to an end is disputed, but usually quoted as c. 1050 BCE.

Hunting

The Shang rulers acted as military leaders, and they and their nobles probably spent a great deal of time hunting. This was a useful way of practising and improving their skills in horsemanship and war. The Shang cavalry was drawn from the ranks of the nobles, who in battle wore bronze helmets and armor made from rhinoceros and buffalo hides. Their preferred weapon was the halberd.

Hunters may have ambushed rhinoceros in narrow valleys and then used spears and halberds, as well as bows and arrows, to bring the animals down.

Bronze wine vessel in the shape of a rhinoceros, from the late Shang period.

Ritual Burial

Later kings of the Shang Dynasty were buried in a large rectangular pit with ramps on each side. The royal coffin was surrounded by the bodies of men and women who were intended to accompany the dead king to the other world. The large tomb was surrounded by smaller pits with dead soldiers, horses, and war chariots. There were also rich grave goods, though the tombs were robbed in ancient times.

This jade figure was found in the tomb of a Shang queen who died in about 1250 BCE. The tomb contained more than 700 jade objects, 500 bone hairpins, and 200 bronze vessels.

Sacrifice

The Shang practised shamanism. Sorcerers and medicine men acted as a link with the supernatural, while diviners used oracle bones to tell fortunes and predict the future. Priest-warriors also carried out ritual human sacrifice, with most of the victims being prisoners of war. Human and animal sacrifices were performed to maintain the goodwill of gods, spirits, and important ancestors.

This bronze axe blade may have been used to execute sacrificial victims.

The Royal Clan

Shang society was based on clans. At the center was the royal clan, named Zi, and other clans became associated with them through marriage, alliance, or conquest. The royal clan was headed by the king, others by warrior nobles. On a king's death, the throne passed to one of his brothers.

This bronze wine vessel was cast for a Shang noble.

Rise of the Zhou

The satellite state of the Zhou overthrew their Shang rulers in the 11th century BCE. The early centuries of the new rule are known as the Western Zhou period because the capital, Hao, was in the west. The Zhou kings ruled wisely, giving authority in their scattered vassal states to junior family members and nobles. This period was looked on by later Chinese philosophers as a golden age of good government and culture.

The Last Shang Capital

After moving their capital, the Shang ended their rule at Anyang. Like the previous capital Zhengzhou, the city was built on a rammed-earth platform, on which there were royal palace buildings. This was surrounded by less important buildings and workshops, as well as a large residential area. In recent years, archeologists have uncovered the foundations of buildings and important tombs beneath the modern city of Anyang.

This bronze wine vessel from the late Shang period shows a tiger protecting a man, who may represent a shaman.

Reconstruction of the royal palace at Anyang, which measured 567 feet (173 m) long and 295 feet (90 m) wide. Remains of burned walls and floors suggest that the palace burned to the ground.

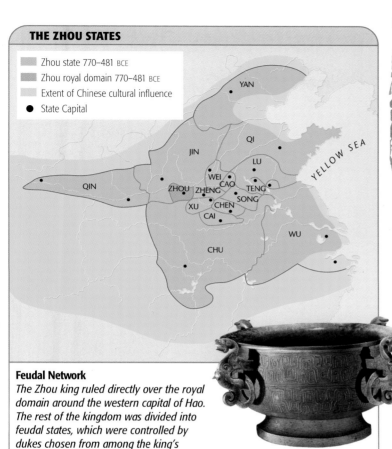

THE ZHOU STATES

- Zhou state 770–481 BCE
- Zhou royal domain 770–481 BCE
- Extent of Chinese cultural influence
- ● State Capital

YAN

QI

JIN

LU

WEI

CAO

ZHOU · ZHENG · TENG

XU · CHEN · SONG

CAI

WU

QIN

CHU

YELLOW SEA

Feudal Network

The Zhou king ruled directly over the royal domain around the western capital of Hao. The rest of the kingdom was divided into feudal states, which were controlled by dukes chosen from among the king's relatives. Each state was run from a fortified city, and the people of neighboring states formed close ties through marriage and shared culture.

This bronze vessel was made to celebrate a royal marriage.

Zhou Origins

The Zhou people, who may have descended from those of the legendary Xia state, came originally from south of the Yellow River. They migrated north, perhaps coming in contact with people of the northern steppes before settling in the valley of the Wei, a tributary of the Yellow River. They gradually expanded eastward toward Shang territory and became one of their satellite states.

Fragment of a silk manuscript of the Yijing (Book of Changes), *a collection of symbolic figures used to predict the future. They were probably collected early in the Zhou period.*

Portrait of King Wu, represented with a statesman's hat and a scholar's robe. According to tradition, King Wu was a hero because he overthrew the last Shang ruler who was an evil tyrant.

Rule and Authority

Zhou rule was based on the powerful authority of the king, who was seen as the "Son of Heaven." This gave him the right to rule over the whole world, so long as he did so justly and with proper concern for his people. The first ruling king after the overthrow of the Shang, Wu, was greatly respected by his people but died shortly after the conquest.

The Zhou made weapons and armour from bronze. This is an early helmet.

The Revolt of King Wu

The Shang kingdom was made up of provinces and vassal states. One of the vassal kings, Wu, from the state of Zhou, formed an alliance with other surrounding states. Meanwhile, the Shang army was becoming weaker and weaker due to wars and expeditions in foreign lands. Taking advantage of this situation, Wu's army was able to overthrow the Shang emperor and establish the longest-lasting dynasty in Chinese history.

The Spring and Autumn Period

The Spring and Autumn period is named after a chronicle of the early Eastern Zhou Dynasty. The capital had moved east from Hao to Luoyang because of "barbarian" attacks. Three centuries of growing disorder followed as central authority and the power of the Zhou dynasty declined. The nobles effectively became the rulers of small independent states, which vied with each other for supremacy. In the 7th century BCE the ruler of the state of Qi took on the title of "overlord."

Above: Bronze statue of a Mongolian girl holding two jade birds. Mongolian nomads were a threat to the northern states.

The Eastern Zhou Period

The Eastern Zhou period was one of a great struggle for supremacy among many small states, after the central power of the dynasty declined. Towns and cities increased in size and number throughout the various regions, and constant warfare meant that important settlements had to be well defended. By the time of the so-called Warring States period, a small number of regions dominated the scene, and all were eventually taken over by the Qin state.

The Warring States Period

By the 5th century BCE, seven important states had become dominant. The southern Chu and western Qin took over much of the former Western Zhou domain, while the northern Jin and eastern Qi absorbed many people who had been outside Zhou influence. But as the states continued to battle with each other, Jin was broken up into three states, the others were taken over by new rulers, and none paid much attention to what was left of the Zhou royal court.

The first coins were miniature implements, such as this bronze knife from the state of Qi.

Chariots were important symbols of power in the Warring States period. These bronze chariot fittings are inlaid with gold.

QIN TERRITORY

ZONGSHAN
YAN
ZHAO
QI
WEI
ZHOU
LU
QIN
XIANYANG •
• LUOYANG
SONG
HAN
SHU
CHU
BA
Yellow River
River Yangzi
YELLOW SEA

Core Qin territory
Qin expansion by 300 BCE
Qin expansion by 220 BCE
Defensive walls

Qin Dominance

By about 350 BCE Qin had become the most powerful state, and its rulers soon adopted the title of king. Qin continued to wage war against the other states, showing great ferocity and military discipline. The Qin ruler, King Zheng, began a series of successful lightning campaigns against neighboring states in 230 BCE.

The Teachings of Confucius

Kongfuzi (c. 551–479 BCE), known as Confucius (a Latin name) was born in the eastern state of Lu. He became a great teacher and philosopher, who committed himself to living in harmony with others and inspiring people to do good. He respected the family as the most important part of society. His ideas—Confucianism—have had enormous influence throughout Chinese society as a guide to morality and good government.

The beliefs of Taoism are based on the teachings of Laozi (c. 570–490 BCE), shown here sitting on a water buffalo. The followers of Confucius saw him as a great philosopher, while others venerated him as a god.

The teachings of Confucius were spread by his disciples, who collected his sayings.

Zhou Music

Music played an important part in Zhou court life, and poems such as those in the *Shijing* (*Book of Songs*) were set to music and performed on ritual occasions. The ancient Chinese believed that music could be a positive, moral force, helping to bring people into harmony. Musical instruments included stone chimes, bronze drums, and bamboo flutes.

This 65-piece set of bronze bells was found in the tomb of a nobleman from the state of Zheng, who died about 433 BCE. The bells were suspended from a lacquered wooden frame and struck with a stick.

The First Empire

By 221 BCE King Zheng of Qin had defeated all the other rival states, and he was able to declare himself Qin Shi Huangdi—the First Sovereign Emperor of Qin. This made him the first ruler of a unified empire; our name for China comes originally from Qin (pronounced "chin"). Qin Shi Huangdi's reign as First Emperor lasted for 11 years, during which time his harsh leadership achieved much. But after his death the Qin Dynasty lost control of the empire in just four years.

Military generals were each given half a token, such as this bronze tiger. An imperial order was only to be obeyed if its messenger carried the other half of the tiger.

Qin Shi Huangdi's Rule

The First Emperor broke up the old Zhou feudal system and replaced it with a centralized government. He divided the empire into 36 administrative units ruled by governors, and forced former rival chiefs to move to his capital, Xianyang. This all-powerful control led Qin Shi Huangdi to prophesy that his empire would last for 10,000 generations. Yet he was deeply superstitious and had a terrible fear of death.

Standardization

In order to make communication quicker and easier, and to improve central control, the Qin Empire was standardized. Weights and measures were unified, along with coinage, and the pictographic writing system was simplified. Qin Shi Huangdi ordered the construction of roads and canals, and even the width of cart and chariot axles was made standard.

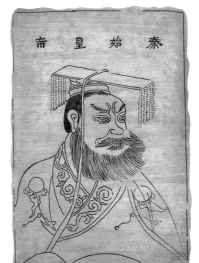

Strict Laws

Qin Shi Huangdi believed in so-called legalist government. This was based on the idea that people are basically undisciplined or even evil. They therefore needed to be kept in order by a combination of strict laws and harsh punishments. The emperor tried to control all knowledge, burning books that disagreed with his system. Scholars who resisted were buried alive, while ordinary citizens were forced into occupations such as farming or the army.

A woodcut of Qin Shi Huangdi.

This bronze model of a horse-drawn chariot was buried near Qin Shi Huangdi's tomb.

The Imperial Guard

After several attempts on his life, Qin Shi Huangdi took steps to protect himself. Each night he slept in a different place, and he and his guards always traveled with more than one carriage. He had a huge tomb complex built, so that he would be protected even after his death. Hundreds of thousands of workers and craftsmen were needed for the complex, which included a model army.

The First Emperor's "terra-cotta army" was made up of more than 7,000 life-sized clay soldiers, along with clay horses and wooden chariots.

Gold buckle of the Xiongnu people, nomads who threatened the new Chinese empire.

The Great Wall

More than 300,000 men were conscripted to join and extend a series of earlier walls that had been built by the conquered states. In this way the emperor wanted to make a continuous barrier against the nomadic northern tribes. The wall was made of pounded earth, and there were garrison stations and signal towers at regular intervals. This was a huge undertaking, and later dynasties maintained and rebuilt the Great Wall in the form that it can still be seen today.

The simple pounded earth wall was rebuilt and restructured by later dynasties. Building the Great Wall—across land that was scorching hot in summer and freezing cold in winter— was desperately hard work.

The Western Han Dynasty

When the Qin official, Liu Bang, defeated his rivals and declared himself Emperor Gaodi in 202 BCE, he took the dynastic title of Han. The name came from the old kingdom that had been conquered by the Qin 28 years earlier. The new Han capital, Changan (modern-day Xian), was on the banks of the Wei River near Xianyang. The so-called Western Han Dynasty ruled uninterrupted for more than 200 years, and during this time the Chinese took up contact with the west, along the famous Silk Road.

Royal Burial
The Han people saw the soul as having two aspects. When a person died, the lighter aspect would go up to the clouds and perhaps join the immortals, while the heavier aspect stayed in the earthly grave. From about 140 BCE, the Han began building tombs in the style of dwellings, often digging them out of cliffs. High-ranking deceased were surrounded by pieces of jade, which were believed to help the soul live forever.

Liu Sheng, son of Emperor Jingdi (reigned 157–141 BCE), and his consort were buried about 113 BCE in suits made from jade plates fastened with gold wire. Their rock-cut tomb included stables, storerooms, and a bathroom.

Han soldiers had to defend their empire against attacks by groups of Xiongnu warriors from the steppes of central Asia and Mongolia. In this scene, Xiongnu horsemen mount a surprise attack on the Great Wall.

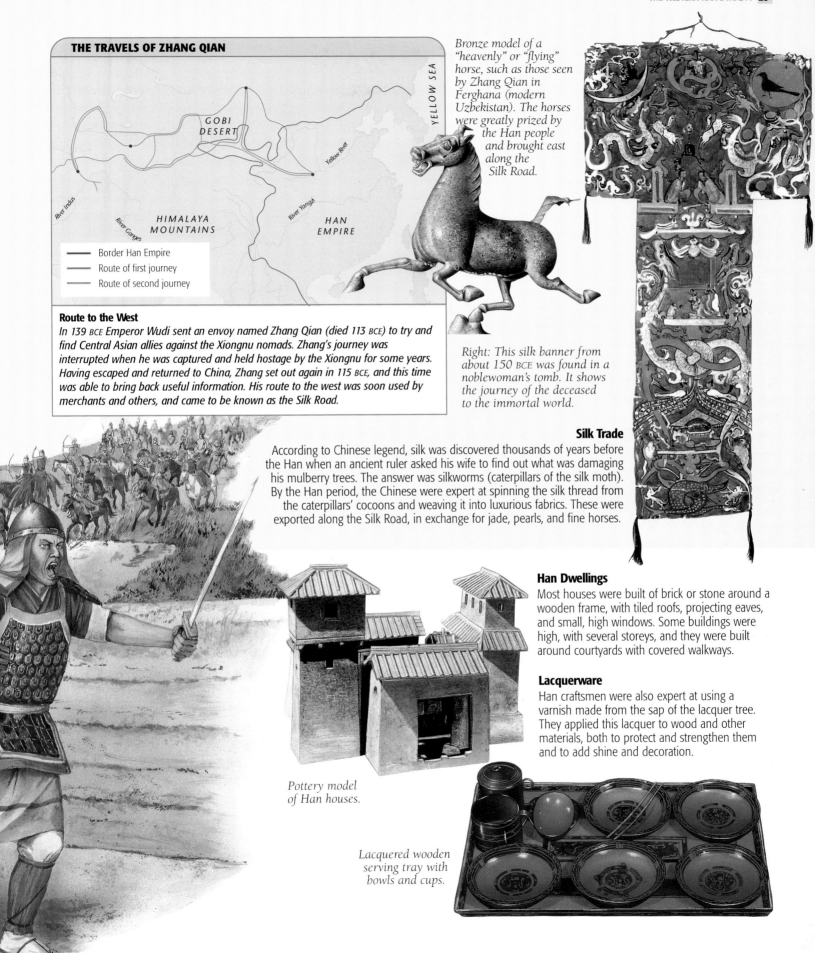

THE TRAVELS OF ZHANG QIAN

GOBI DESERT

YELLOW SEA

Yellow River

River Indus

River Ganges

HIMALAYA MOUNTAINS

River Yangzi

HAN EMPIRE

— Border Han Empire
— Route of first journey
— Route of second journey

Route to the West

In 139 BCE Emperor Wudi sent an envoy named Zhang Qian (died 113 BCE) to try and find Central Asian allies against the Xiongnu nomads. Zhang's journey was interrupted when he was captured and held hostage by the Xiongnu for some years. Having escaped and returned to China, Zhang set out again in 115 BCE, and this time was able to bring back useful information. His route to the west was soon used by merchants and others, and came to be known as the Silk Road.

Bronze model of a "heavenly" or "flying" horse, such as those seen by Zhang Qian in Ferghana (modern Uzbekistan). The horses were greatly prized by the Han people and brought east along the Silk Road.

Right: This silk banner from about 150 BCE was found in a noblewoman's tomb. It shows the journey of the deceased to the immortal world.

Silk Trade

According to Chinese legend, silk was discovered thousands of years before the Han when an ancient ruler asked his wife to find out what was damaging his mulberry trees. The answer was silkworms (caterpillars of the silk moth). By the Han period, the Chinese were expert at spinning the silk thread from the caterpillars' cocoons and weaving it into luxurious fabrics. These were exported along the Silk Road, in exchange for jade, pearls, and fine horses.

Han Dwellings

Most houses were built of brick or stone around a wooden frame, with tiled roofs, projecting eaves, and small, high windows. Some buildings were high, with several storeys, and they were built around courtyards with covered walkways.

Lacquerware

Han craftsmen were also expert at using a varnish made from the sap of the lacquer tree. They applied this lacquer to wood and other materials, both to protect and strengthen them and to add shine and decoration.

Pottery model of Han houses.

Lacquered wooden serving tray with bowls and cups.

Wang Mang

In 9 CE a distant relative of the imperial Liu family took over from the 4-year-old Ruzi and declared himself emperor. Wang Mang named his dynasty Xin (meaning "New"), but the founder was to be the only Xin emperor. During his reign he attacked the privileges of wealthy landowners and tried to abolish private slave-ownership, but met with great opposition.

Rebellion

Rebel groups rose up against the rule of Wang Mang, and the emperor received no help from the wealthy classes. In 23 CE there was fighting in the streets of Changan, and rebels broke through to the imperial palace. Wang Mang and his attendants were killed.

Stone relief showing a Han farmer using an ox-drawn plow.

Xin dynasty tortoise-topped seal and its imprint.

The Eastern Han Dynasty

For a period of 16 years after 9 CE, the rule of the Han Dynasty was interrupted by rebellion, civil war, and the reign of Xin emperor Wang Mang. When Han power had been regained, 12 emperors of the so-called Eastern Han Dynasty ruled for almost 200 years. During this period government was less centralized, as farming methods improved, trade flourished, and merchants and landowners grew rich and powerful. Power struggles at court eventually weakened the empire.

Salt Wells

Salt was important for preserving meat and fish, and in Han times people developed new methods of obtaining it. Around the area of Zigong, north of the Yangzi, workers sank wells using percussion drills—pointed tools that were dropped or hammered down bamboo tubes —to recover brine. The liquid was boiled in large vats, leaving behind high-quality salt.

At the salt well, tall wooden derricks were put up as a framework to support the drill. Natural gas was burned to boil the brine.

Moving East and South

The city of Changan was ruined during the rebellion and civil war that followed, and Han emperor Guang Wudi moved the capital east to Luoyang in the lower Yellow River Valley. Luoyang was much smaller than Changan and soon became very crowded. Though imperial power was in the east during this period, there was also a great movement of the population towards the south. In the Yangzi Valley, irrigation schemes meant that rice production increased dramatically.

This bronze standard measure, introduced by Wang Mang, has five separate measuring parts.

EASTERN HAN

9–25 CE
Reign of Wang Mang, who founds the Xin ("new") dynasty.

11 CE
Yellow River changes course and causes disastrous floods.

25–57 CE
Reign of Liu Xiu, a descendant of earlier Han emperor Jingdi, as Guang Wudi ("Shining Martial Emperor").

25–220 CE
Eastern (or Later) Han period; capital moved to the east (Luoyang).

c. 100 CE
First Chinese dictionary is compiled, explaining more than 9,000 characters.

c. 105 CE
Paper comes into use.

126 CE
Peasant revolts against landowners.

150 CE
Buddhism reaches China.

184 CE
Uprising by the Taoist Yellow Turban rebel group.

189–220 CE
Reign of the last Han emperor, Xiandi.

Han coins grow magically on this bronze "money tree."

Clay sculpture of a storyteller beating a drum.

Decline of the Han

During the reign of Huandi (146–168), there were many natural disasters —floods, earthquakes, plagues of locusts, drought, and resulting famine. Over the next 50 years the Han Dynasty lost power, as their administration became corrupt. Provincial officials gained power, rivalry between imperial relatives and the court's eunuchs led to violence, and eventually regional warlords had more authority than the emperor. In 220 CE the last Han emperor handed over power.

Agriculture

The ancient Chinese economy was based on agriculture. Farming families had high status in theory, because they were so important to the empire, but they had very hard lives. Peasants paid a large part of their earnings to rich landowners or to the state in taxes. In the dry north, where the land was difficult to work, there were smaller farms and families looked after themselves. In the more fertile south, families worked for others on larger farming estates.

These hard-working men and women are shown bringing in the rice harvest.

Chinese Civilization

Ancient Chinese rulers were seen as passing on the "mandate of heaven," or divine authority, through their sons to their descendants and future dynasties. The empire's subjects were divided into orderly classes according to Confucian tradition, with the majority working on the land, and a new element was added with the introduction of Buddhist culture. Despite the many battles, civil wars and periods of disunity, the resulting Chinese civilization was highly successful, producing great scientists, scholars, craftsmen, and artists.

Confucian Society

According to the Confucian view of the world that ruled after the 5th century BCE, society could be divided into four main groups. At the top were educated scholars, nobles and landowners; next came hard-working peasants; third were skilled workers and craftsmen; and at the bottom of the social scale were merchants. This scale was based on the importance of individuals to the whole population.

Confucius taught the importance of respect for parents and the family. This wicker basket of the Eastern Han period is painted with scenes of men showing respect for their parents.

Papermaking

Paper was invented in ancient China, probably during the 2nd century BCE, when it was made from hemp and other fibres. Before that texts were written on strips of wood or bamboo, and also on silk. In 105 CE the invention of paper was officially reported to the emperor, and after that date papermakers used the bark of certain plants to make paper that was stronger and finer. The Chinese kept the art of papermaking a secret for several centuries.

A fragment of paper from the 2nd century CE.

Board used to play liubo, *an entertaining game which was sometimes played to predict the future.*

Ink was valued by ancient scholars. This ink container is made of gilt bronze inlaid with turquoise.

Trade

Though they were supposedly at the bottom of the social scale, merchants were successful and became rich. They used a growing network of roads and canals to move goods within the empire. To the west, the desert routes of the Silk Road linked oases and trading settlements all the way to central Asia and beyond. Individual merchants did not accompany their caravans the whole way, but simply took their goods to the next stage, where they sold or exchanged them.

Science and Technology

Astronomy was an early science in China, and ancient astronomers carved a detailed star chart of the heavens on a stone mound in about 3000 BCE. Later scholars studied mathematics and medicine, including forms of acupuncture that are still used today. Scientists also made many practical inventions, such as the wheelbarrow in the 2nd century CE.

Ceramic model of an ox cart, which was a common means of transport.

This seismoscope, invented by a Chinese astronomer in 132 CE, warned of earthquakes and their location. An Earth tremor would cause a dragon to drop a bronze ball into a waiting toad's mouth.

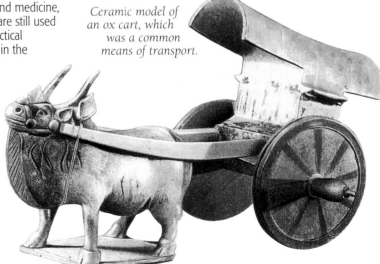

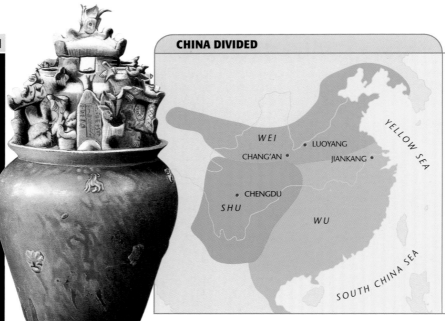

This pottery spirit jar has a miniature shrine on its lid in honor of clan ancestors.

The Jin Dynasties

In 265 CE the Wei throne was taken by one of the kingdom's generals, Wudi (reigned 265–289 CE), who founded the Western Jin Dynasty. Fifteen years later, the Wu Kingdom was also defeated and the Western Jin emperor, Wudi, briefly reunited China. After conflicts within the imperial family and many attacks by northern steppe tribes, including the sacking of Luoyang and Changan, Jin leaders fled south-east. In 317 CE Yuandi (reigned 317–322 CE) established the Eastern Jin Dynasty, with its court at Jiankang.

CHINA DIVIDED

WEI

CHANG'AN • • LUOYANG

JIANKANG •

• CHENGDU

SHU

WU

YELLOW SEA

SOUTH CHINA SEA

The Three Kingdoms
The most powerful kingdom was Wei, which lay around the Yellow River Valley. Its first emperor was Wei Wendi (reigned 220–226), the son of the warlord Cao Cao (155–220 CE), protector of the last Han emperor. The western Shu Kingdom was the first to fall, when its capital, Chengdu, was captured by the Wei. The rulers of the large Wu Kingdom, to the south, had no historic links to the Han clan. Chinese historians generally regard the Wei as the official imperial line.

The Period of Disunion

After the collapse of the Eastern Han Dynasty, China was first divided into three kingdoms. Threats from steppe nomads continued in the north, and they eventually united under northern dynasties, though these are not recognised by Chinese historians. In the south, a series of dynasties reigned over a region where calligraphy, painting and literature flourished. China was finally reunited in 589 CE under another new dynasty, the Sui.

Spread of Buddhism

Buddhist beliefs and practices spread throughout the Chinese region during this period. People paid less attention to traditional Confucian views of society, and by the 4th century CE Buddhism was the dominant religion. Buddhist missionaries and merchants from India also brought ideas about sculpture and painting that had a great impact on Chinese artists.

Lion-shaped pottery lamp-holder from the Western Jin period.

This Chinese gilt-bronze Buddha, dating from 338 CE, was based on a formal Indian style.

Young ladies of the court were guided by an instructress who dictated the correct rules of behavior.

Life at Court

During the time of the Eastern Jin, there was a great flowering of the arts, especially around the capital Jiankang. At court and elsewhere, women were expected to behave with great decorum. As well as enjoying the company of the empress and secondary wives, the emperor surrounded himself with young women who were given the titles "honorable lady," "beautiful lady" or "chosen lady."

A court official wears the cylindrical hat of a noble courtier.

A 5th-century CE dragon-shaped jade pendant from southern China. Since the north was threatened by invasion of foreigners, the cultural center of China moved to the south.

North and South

In the late 4th century CE nomadic people of Turkic origin took over the entire northern region. Their rule has come to be known as the Northern Dynasties period. In the south, the first of the so-called Southern Dynasties—the Liu Song—took over from the Jin and continued the Han tradition. By the end of the 5th century CE, the non-Han northern rulers had taken up much of traditional Chinese culture.

The Founding Legend

According to legend, the first Korean ruler was Tangun, who became king of Choson in 2333 BCE. Grandson of the creator god Hwanin, he was the son of divine King Hwanung and a she-bear that had magically turned into a woman. There are several different versions of the legend, which is important to many Koreans because it links their state with a heavenly origin.

An illustration of one version of the legend of Tangun, which includes a tiger with the bear.

Dolmens

As in other parts of the world, simple stone structures were placed over many burials in ancient Korea. These tomb structures, called dolmens, were of different types. In the north, many were of the table type, with a large capstone raised high off the ground. In the south, the capstone often rested on smaller stones at ground level. The dolmens may have been seen as status symbols.

This table-type dolmen stands about 8 feet (2.5 m) high.

Ancient Korea

The Korean peninsula lies to the northeast of China, and its early history was greatly influenced by its Chinese neighbors. In ancient times, and especially after its Bronze Age began around 1000 BCE, the peninsula had several small tribal states. The most advanced was Choson, which grew up around the Taedong River, near modern Pyongyang. Several other states emerged, before the peninsula was finally united as the Kingdom of Silla in 676 CE.

Comb-Pattern Pottery

Around 7,000 years ago, the region's potters were putting together coils of clay to make wide-mouthed storage and cooking vessels with a pointed or round base. Before firing the pots, they decorated the damp clay with patterns of diagonal lines. They may have used a comb-like tool to achieve this.

This large comb-pattern pot, dating from about 3500 BCE, was found near the River Han in modern-day Seoul.

Underfloor Heating

In ancient times (perhaps as early as the 4th century BCE), the Koreans began heating their wooden houses with an ingenious underfloor system. This was called *ondol*, meaning "warm stone." It worked by directing hot air and smoke from a wood-burning stove through pipes beneath the floor, before releasing them through outdoor chimneys. Today, the Korean *ondol* system works by pumping hot water through underfloor pipes.

ANCIENT KOREA

KOGURYO

• KUNGNAESONG

SEA OF JAPAN

• LELANG

SILLA

KYONGJU •

YELLOW SEA

PUYO •

PAEKCHE

- ☐ Wei Kingdom
- ☐ Yayoi culture 300 CE
- — Yamato Kingdom 300 CE
- ☐ The Three Kingdoms
- ● Capital city 220-581 CE

Three Kingdoms

Beginning in the 1st century CE (though the traditional dates are much earlier), Korean tribes came together to form the kingdoms of Koguryo, Paekche, and Silla. This period in Korean history is known as the Three Kingdoms. The northern kingdom of Koguryo was the largest, and its king built a strong army, which eventually drove the Chinese from Lelang. All three kingdoms developed advanced cultures.

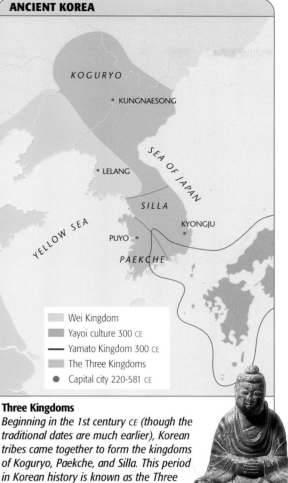

Soft stone Buddha from Paekche. Buddhism was introduced to the Three Kingdoms during the 4th century CE.

Han Invasion

In 108 BCE, during the reign of the Han emperor Wudi (see pages 28–29), the Chinese invaded and conquered much of the Korean peninsula. The Chinese organized their new territory into four military districts. Korean tribesmen succeeded in winning back three of these districts by 75 BCE, but the fourth Chinese colony, called Lelang (or Luolang), lasted for over 400 years.

Reconstruction of ironworking in Korea after the Han invasion. With a longer tradition of ironworking, the Chinese helped improve Korean technology.

Early Japan

The ancient Japanese are credited with making the world's first pottery, more than 12,000 years ago. A hunter-gatherer culture, called Jomon after its style of pottery, developed near the coast. This flourished for thousands of years, until the skills of rice-growing and ironworking were introduced from the Asian mainland and changed ways of life. People of the Yayoi culture lived in settled farming villages, which in time came to be controlled by local chieftains.

Reconstruction of a Jomon pit house. There was a sunken floor inside.

Early Settlements

People of the early Jomon culture lived in pit houses clustered together in groups, probably in a circle. Early settlements may have been made up of about 50 people. The floor of each dwelling was dug into the ground, and a wooden framework supported walls and roof. People lived by hunting and gathering, especially by fishing and shellfish-collecting near the coast.

This Jomon (or cord-marked) pot dates from about 2500 BCE. The pottery and period take their name from the method of decorating damp clay pots with cord or plant fibres before baking them in an open fire. Early Jomon potters were probably women.

Shinto

People of the Jomon culture lived close to nature and had great respect for natural forms and forces. Their beliefs contributed to the ancient Japanese religion of Shinto, which means the "way of the gods." These gods were the spirits of nature, such as the forces present in animals, plants, mountains, seas, storms, and earthquakes. Shinto had no founder or scriptures. Its followers saw the legendary first emperor, Jimmu Tennō, as a descendant of the sun goddess Amaterasu.

Mount Fuji, a dormant volcano and the highest mountain in Japan, has always been sacred to the followers of Shinto.

Burial Jars

During the Yayoi period, clay jars were used for burials. Children were usually placed in a single jar, while adults were buried in large paired jars that were sealed together with clay. Graves were marked by mounds of earth or stone slabs, and many were placed close together in large cemeteries. Precious objects were placed in or near some jar burials.

From this period chieftains were buried with "three sacred treasures" —a sword, mirror, and jewel. This bronze sword and mirror, along with the jade jewel, come from a Yayoi tomb.

An adult paired jar burial.

Rice

Wet-rice agriculture was introduced during the middle of the 1st millennium BCE. Beginning on the southern island of Kyushu, methods of growing rice in irrigated fields gradually spread to the main island of Honshu. This led to a new culture, based on farming rather than foraging. We call this culture Yayoi, from the name of the village where pottery and other remains were first found.

Finds of carbonized grains of rice such as these tell archeologists about farming in ancient times.

THE SPREAD OF YAYOI CULTURE

- Yayoi culture 100 BCE
- Spread of Yayoi culture 100 BCE – 100 CE
- Spread of Yayoi culture after 100 CE
- Han Empire c. 108 BCE
- State capital

KOGURYO
LELANG
SEA OF JAPAN
MT. FUJI
NOBI
IZUMO
KINAI ASUKA
KIBI
PAEKCHE
PUYO
SILLA
KNONGJU
YAMATO
KONGIU
KAYA
NORTHERN KYUSHU
SAITOBARU
YELLOW SEA
PACIFIC OCEAN

The Yayoi Period

During this period local chieftains began to gain control over larger territories. Bronze and iron weapons and tools were imported from the Asian mainland from about 300 BCE. Over the next few centuries Yayoi craftsmen learned how to produce and work both metals. They were used for practical purposes, as well as for making ceremonial and ritual objects.

The Daisen burial mound in the city of Sakai. This keyhole-shaped mound is 1,594 feet (486 m) long.

Later version of a page from the Kojiki or "Record of Ancient Matters." This was originally written in 712 CE using Chinese characters with added Japanese kana symbols.

Burial Mounds

Mound-covered tombs became more elaborate during this period. By the 5th century CE the largest had a keyhole-shaped mound, surrounded by rows of small pottery objects (called *haniwa*) and one or more moats. Beneath the mound was a stone-lined burial chamber with a stone sarcophagus, as well as swords and other grave goods.

This haniwa *takes the form of a young soldier kneeling in respect. These pottery figures may have been seen as military guardians for the deceased.*

Chinese Influence

Early in the 5th century CE, the Chinese system of pictographic writing was brought to Japan from Korea. The Japanese adopted the Chinese system, which they called *kanji* and which was used by courtiers and other educated people. A few centuries later, a system of Japanese pronunciation symbols was added, called *kana*.

The Kofun Period

The period of Japanese history from the 4th to the 6th century CE is known as the Kofun period. The name comes from the distinctive large burial mounds (*kofun*, or "old tombs," in Japanese). During this period, powerful clans began to dominate others and form states or kingdoms. The Yamato Kingdom, named after a region on the Nara plain of Honshu, became the most powerful and wealthy state. The dominant Yamato clan took control over a large area and founded the imperial line of Japan.

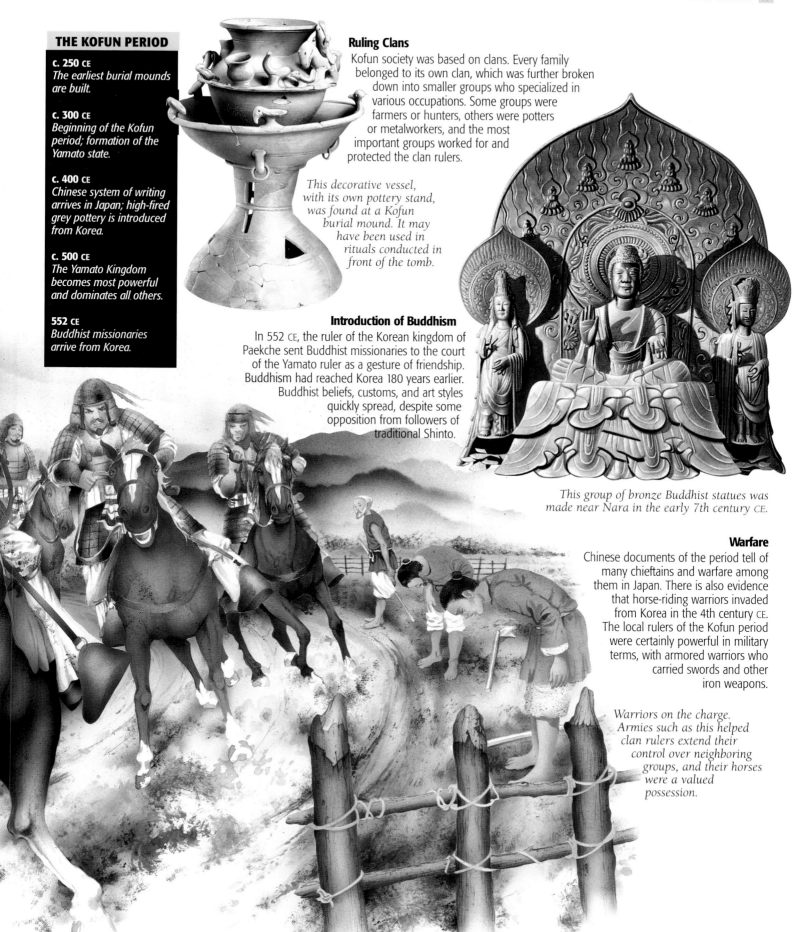

THE KOFUN PERIOD

c. 250 CE
The earliest burial mounds are built.

c. 300 CE
Beginning of the Kofun period; formation of the Yamato state.

c. 400 CE
Chinese system of writing arrives in Japan; high-fired grey pottery is introduced from Korea.

c. 500 CE
The Yamato Kingdom becomes most powerful and dominates all others.

552 CE
Buddhist missionaries arrive from Korea.

Ruling Clans

Kofun society was based on clans. Every family belonged to its own clan, which was further broken down into smaller groups who specialized in various occupations. Some groups were farmers or hunters, others were potters or metalworkers, and the most important groups worked for and protected the clan rulers.

This decorative vessel, with its own pottery stand, was found at a Kofun burial mound. It may have been used in rituals conducted in front of the tomb.

Introduction of Buddhism

In 552 CE, the ruler of the Korean kingdom of Paekche sent Buddhist missionaries to the court of the Yamato ruler as a gesture of friendship. Buddhism had reached Korea 180 years earlier. Buddhist beliefs, customs, and art styles quickly spread, despite some opposition from followers of traditional Shinto.

This group of bronze Buddhist statues was made near Nara in the early 7th century CE.

Warfare

Chinese documents of the period tell of many chieftains and warfare among them in Japan. There is also evidence that horse-riding warriors invaded from Korea in the 4th century CE. The local rulers of the Kofun period were certainly powerful in military terms, with armored warriors who carried swords and other iron weapons.

Warriors on the charge. Armies such as this helped clan rulers extend their control over neighboring groups, and their horses were a valued possession.

EARLY SOUTHEAST ASIA

c. 6000 BCE
The first farming settlements; the first pottery on the mainland.

c. 2500 BCE
The first pottery and domesticated animals on the islands.

c. 2000 BCE
Use of bronze in Thailand; Phung Nyugen culture with rice cultivation in the Red River Valley, Vietnam.

1500–1000 BCE
Dong Dau bronze-working culture in Vietnam.

1000–500 BCE
Go Mun bronze-working culture in Vietnam.

c. 700 BCE
The first use of iron in the region.

700 BCE
Beginnings of Dong Son bronze and iron-working culture in Vietnam.

c. 300 BCE
Early form of writing, based on Sanskrit from India, is used in Cambodia.

250 BCE
The first walled settlements (in Vietnam).

c. 200 BCE
Water buffalo used as a draught animal.

SOUTHEAST ASIA IN PREHISTORY

● Ancient site

TAUNGTHAMAN
Irrawaddy
Red River
BANG CHIANG
DONG SONG
SOUTH CHINA SEA
Mekong
MALAY PENINSULA
SUMATRA
BORNEO
SULAWESI
INDIAN OCEAN
JAVA

Archeological Sites
In prehistoric times there were large movements of people throughout the region, as increasing populations looked for fresh sources of food. This map shows some of the important archeological sites of Southeast Asia. Most of the interesting discoveries on the mainland of Myanmar, Thailand, and Vietnam (at Taungthaman, Bang Chang, and Dong Song) were first made during the 20th century.

Stone bracelet from a burial site at Taungthaman, beside the River Irrawaddy.

Stone Age Migration
We believe that the first farmers of the region came from tribal groups that migrated south from China down great rivers such as the Irrawaddy. Some of these groups may have carried on their nomadic hunting and gathering way of life, while others settled in the river valleys of present-day Myanmar and developed methods of cultivating rice. In the settlements they made elaborate stone tools and built a strong farming culture.

Red spiral patterns decorate this pot from Ban Chiang, which dates from around 300 BCE.

Civilizations of Southeast Asia

Ban Chiang
Decorative pottery, bronze objects, and elaborate burial offerings have been found at the settlement of Ban Chiang, in the northeast of present-day Thailand. The settlement was beside a tributary of the Mekong River, where people were smelting and casting bronze from about 2000 BCE. Many historians believe that this technology developed separately in the region rather than being introduced from elsewhere.

As in other parts of the world, the early people of the Southeast Asian mainland and islands used stone to make increasingly sophisticated tools and weapons. Some of those who settled in the fertile river valleys began making bronze, and its use spread throughout the region. Early bronze drums have been found on the islands of Sumatra and Borneo, as well as in the modern mainland countries and southern China. Pottery was another early development.

A carved megalith found on an island off Sumatra, Indonesia.

This bronze Dong Son model drum dates from some time after 300 BCE. It represents larger bronze drums that may have been played at religious ceremonies, to rally men for battle, or even to encourage rain.

This hollowed-log coffin dates from the Dong Son period. The deceased was buried with a spear, axe heads, a bamboo ladle, and pottery vessel at his feet, all for use in the afterlife.

Bronze Dong Son lamp-holder in the form of a kneeling man with a bowl.

Dong Son Culture

The settlement of Dong Son, on the plain south of the Red River Valley (and present-day Hanoi) in northern Vietnam, has given its name to a culture of the late Bronze Age and early Iron Age. Most of the tools and weapons found at the site and in the surrounding region were made of bronze. Burial places contained ritual and personal objects such as ceremonial daggers, buckles, musical instruments, and drums.

Trade with India

Iron appeared in the region around 700 BCE, and many experts believe that it was worked locally. However, there is evidence that items such as beads of glass, agate, and carnelian were acquired by trade from India, which leads some historians to think that the earliest iron objects appeared in the same way.

Carnelian and agate necklace from western Thailand (4th century BCE). Its Indian style suggests it was acquired by trade.

SOUTHEAST ASIA

100 CE
The Pyu establish kingdoms in Myanmar; the kingdom of Funan is founded in the lower Mekong Valley (present-day Cambodia and Vietnam); metalwork begins on the region's islands.

200 CE
Indian ceramics are in use on the island of Bali.

c. 200–400 CE
Spread of Buddhist influence from India; Peikthano is an important Buddhist center in Myanmar.

300 CE
The kingdom of Funan reaches the height of its power; the Dong Son culture loses influence.

400 CE
The Pyu reach the height of their power.

400–500CE
Sanskrit inscriptions appear on the islands of Borneo and Java.

Reconstruction of a riverside village. The horned shape of some of the roofs might have represented the buffalo. The animal was seen as a link between heaven and earth.

Stilt Village

Most villagers probably lived in houses that were raised by stilts 6–10 feet (2–3 m) above ground, which prevented flooding in riverside and coastal settlements. The remains of ancient post holes confirm this, and many of the native peoples of the region still live traditionally in the same way. The raised floors were made of strips of wood placed side by side, the walls may have been of tree bark, and the roofs were thatched.

From Village to Kingdom

During the 1st millennium CE, some early villages in Southeast Asia grew into large urban settlements and city-kingdoms. The entire region was greatly influenced by contact with India, and to a lesser extent China. This applied to the islands that make up present-day Indonesia, as well as the mainland. Local rulers adopted Indian customs, Hindu and Buddhist styles influenced art and architecture, and Sanskrit also had its influence on the region's languages.

Chinese junks such as this sailed across the South China Sea to the Southeast Asian mainland and islands.

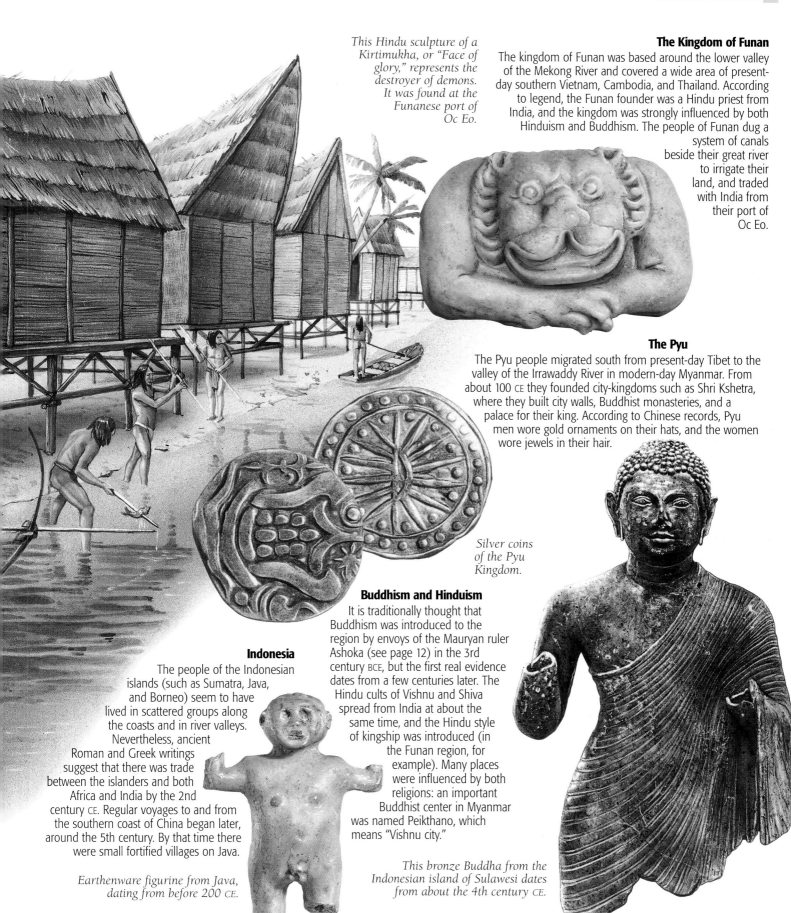

This Hindu sculpture of a Kirtimukha, or "Face of glory," represents the destroyer of demons. It was found at the Funanese port of Oc Eo.

The Kingdom of Funan

The kingdom of Funan was based around the lower valley of the Mekong River and covered a wide area of present-day southern Vietnam, Cambodia, and Thailand. According to legend, the Funan founder was a Hindu priest from India, and the kingdom was strongly influenced by both Hinduism and Buddhism. The people of Funan dug a system of canals beside their great river to irrigate their land, and traded with India from their port of Oc Eo.

The Pyu

The Pyu people migrated south from present-day Tibet to the valley of the Irrawaddy River in modern-day Myanmar. From about 100 CE they founded city-kingdoms such as Shri Kshetra, where they built city walls, Buddhist monasteries, and a palace for their king. According to Chinese records, Pyu men wore gold ornaments on their hats, and the women wore jewels in their hair.

Silver coins of the Pyu Kingdom.

Buddhism and Hinduism

It is traditionally thought that Buddhism was introduced to the region by envoys of the Mauryan ruler Ashoka (see page 12) in the 3rd century BCE, but the first real evidence dates from a few centuries later. The Hindu cults of Vishnu and Shiva spread from India at about the same time, and the Hindu style of kingship was introduced (in the Funan region, for example). Many places were influenced by both religions: an important Buddhist center in Myanmar was named Peikthano, which means "Vishnu city."

Indonesia

The people of the Indonesian islands (such as Sumatra, Java, and Borneo) seem to have lived in scattered groups along the coasts and in river valleys. Nevertheless, ancient Roman and Greek writings suggest that there was trade between the islanders and both Africa and India by the 2nd century CE. Regular voyages to and from the southern coast of China began later, around the 5th century. By that time there were small fortified villages on Java.

Earthenware figurine from Java, dating from before 200 CE.

This bronze Buddha from the Indonesian island of Sulawesi dates from about the 4th century CE.

Glossary

Acupuncture A method of treating disease and easing pain by inserting needles in certain parts of the body.

Alloy A mixture of two or more different metals, usually to make a new or stronger metal. Bronze, which is made by the mixture, or alloying, of copper and tin, is stronger and easier to work than copper.

Amulet An object or charm that is worn by a person because it is believed to keep away bad luck or evil.

Archeologist A scientist who studies the remains of ancient peoples, such as tools, weapons, pots, and buildings, to learn more about cultures of the distant past.

Astronomy The scientific study of the Sun, Moon, and stars and other heavenly bodies.

Barbarian Term used in a negative way, meaning rude or uncivilized, to describe any foreigners or people who do not share a similar culture.

Brine Water which contains a large amount of salt.

Bronze Age The period in human development following the Stone Age in which people used bronze to make weapons and tools. One of the Metal Ages.

Citadel A fortress or an armed, commanding city built to function as a place of safety and defence.

Clan A group of people belonging to the same tribe who are related or share a common ancestor.

Crop A plant or its product, such as grain, fruit, or vegetables, grown by farmers.

Decorum Behavior or appearance that follows the customs or rules of a society or culture.

Diviner A person believed to have the ability to tell the future.

Dolmen A simple structure made of upright stones which support a large stone slab.

Domesticate To tame and bring animals and plants under control so that they can live with and serve people.

Dynasty A line of rulers coming from the same family, or a period during which they reign.

Envoy A messenger sent by a government on a special mission and who acts as a representative of the government or state.

Epic A long poem which tells the story of gods and heroes or the history of a nation or people.

Eunuch A man who had part of his sex organs removed and served in the courts of emperors.

Feudal system A social organization in which people held and worked the land owned by a lord who demanded military service in return.

Forage To search for and collect food.

Geometric Term used to describe something decorated with or having the form of simple shapes such as squares, triangles, and circles.

Halberd A combined spear and battleaxe.

Iron Age The period in human development following the Bronze Age in which people used iron to make weapons and tools. One of the Metal Ages.

Irrigation The process of bringing water to fields.

Kiln An oven used for baking, hardening, or drying materials such as grain, clay, or ceramics.

Megalith A huge stone, usually standing, used in the construction of prehistoric monuments.

Missionary One who is sent on a mission to a foreign land to educate or convert people to a particular religion.

Molten Melted, or in a liquid state under a very high temperature.

Morality A set of principles based on cultural and or religious beliefs by which a person judges if an action is right or wrong. The following of a system of rules of behavior.

Nomad A member of a tribe that travels from place to place in search of pastures for animals. A person who wanders and does not settle down in any particular place.

Oracle A sacred place where questions about the future are answered. A person, such as a priest or a priestess, who speaks for a god, answering questions about future events, usually in riddles.

Pictograph A picture representing a word or idea.

Plain A vast or large, flat, area of land, usually without trees.

Province One of many divisions of a state made by a government to have better control over the territory.

Relic An object that has survived from the past and is kept for its spiritual or historical significance. A sacred object, such as a part of the body or an object, that once belonged to a holy person.

Sanctuary A sacred, holy place or temple.

Sarcophagus A container made to store dead bodies, usually made of stone.

Satellite state A country that is under the economic, political, and military control of a larger, more powerful neighboring country.

Shaman A priest who is believed to be able to contact the spirit world and who practices magic to heal, predict the future, and control natural events.

Smelt To melt down earth (or an ore) in order to separate and extract its metallic parts.

Sovereign A ruler who has complete control or the most power over a state or country.

Steppe One of the large areas of flat, tree-less land of southeastern Europe and Siberia.

Stone Age The early period in human development preceding the Metal Ages in which people used only stone to make weapons and tools.

Stupa A dome-shaped monument built to store Buddhist relics.

Tributary A stream that flows into a river or a larger body of water.

Index